Chameleon Care

The Complete Guide to Caring for and
Keeping Chameleons as Pets

Tabitha Jones

ISBN: 9781798946558

CONTENTS

INTRODUCTION

Before purchasing any pet it is important to understand that as a pet owner you are responsible for the care and wellbeing of your pet. It is important to try and learn as much as you can about the animal you are considering to keep as a pet to make sure that your lifestyle, household and financial status are suited to provide your pet with the best possible care. This guide has been designed to provide you with both precise and concise information about a chameleon's basic needs to help you provide your pet with the best quality care practices.

DESCRIPTION

Chameleons (who belong to the Chamaeleonidae family) are a highly unique clade of reptile which originate from Africa, Europe and Asia. In the present day, chameleons can be often found in warm habitats that range from rain forests to deserts and can be found throughout Africa, Madagascar, southern Europe (near the equator), southern Asia and they have even been introduced to Hawaii, California and Florida. There are over 200 recognized species of chameleon which means they come in a wide variety of sizes and colour morphs. Chameleons are adapted for visual hunting and climbing. They have multiple specialized features which help them hunt and avoid predators which include their ability to camouflage themselves by changing their color, their zygodactylous feet, their prehensile tail and their independently mobile eyes. All of the aforementioned specialized features will be discussed in a separate section of this care manual.

Size

As previously stated there are hundreds of different species of chameleon and the sizes of the different species are therefore varied. The smallest species of chameleon, the male *'Brookesia micra'* can be as small as 15mm in length. The largest species of chameleon is the male *'Furcifer oustaleti'* which can be as long as 70cm in length!

Natural Habitat

Chameleons can be found in a wide range of different habitats. They are most commonly found in tropical and mountain rain forests and savannas. It is also not uncommon for certain species of chameleon to be found in desert and savanna habitats. The majority of chameleon species are arboreal (which means they live primarily in trees) but a few of the larger species are terrestrial (which means they resided and live on the ground). Sadly in recent years there has been a decline in the wild chameleon population due to deforestation and pollution.

Lifespan

Chameleons in the wild will normally live for around 2 or 3 years. However in captivity, due to the safe environment and regular feeding, chameleons normally live between 3 and 10 years!

Differences between the Sexes

It is possible to distinguish between male and female chameleons based upon the appearance of their back feet. A male veiled chameleon will always have a pad, known as a spur, on both of its hind feet. There is no noticeable temperament differences between the sexes as chameleons seem to always have their own individual personality. It is important to consider that a female chameleon will become 'gravid,' or full, of eggs up to three times a year and if this process if not catered for properly the female may become 'egg bound' which can be a serious threat to her life. If you do not wish to deal with this process it is best practice to purchase a male chameleon.

Diet

Chameleons are insectivores which means that their diet consists primarily of insects. A wild chameleon's diet will mainly consist of a variety of insects and other small invertebrates such as worms and arachnids. It is also not uncommon for certain species of chameleon to eat plants and other vegetation.

UNIQUE FEATURES OF THE CHAMELEON

As previously mentioned chameleons have multiple specialized features which help them in the wild to escape predator, catch prey and survive. These interesting specialized feature add to the species' desirability as pets. The following section will explain some of these features in more detail.

Zygodactylous Feet

Chameleons are the only reptile with zygodactylous feet – the only other animals with this type of feet are birds. Chameleons have two toes facing forward and two toes facing backwards. This toe arrangement allows chameleons to gain a sturdy grasp of tree branches and makes them particularly good climbers. Their unique feet also help them avoid predators as they can remain stationary on a branch for prolonged periods of time as well as helping them hunt their prey in the trees.

Prehensile Tail

Most larger species of chameleon have a prehensile tail. The chameleons prehensile tail allows them to hang from tree branches due to the fact that their tail can grasp onto the branch. The prehensile tail allows the chameleon to have a great natural advantage over lizards in their ecosystems due to the fact that they can manipulate their bodies into positions that other lizards cannot achieve.

Independent Eyes

Chameleons' eyes are able to move independently of each other. Due to the ability to move both eyes independently chameleons have approximately 360 degree vision which is both a great defensive tool and predatory tool. Chameleons also synchronize their eyes to give them better aim when hunting their prey. When a Chameleon targets a cricket, locust or meal worm it will turn its head to face the prey. The Chameleon will then point both eyes directly at the target, switching to stereoscopic or binocular vision. The Chameleon uses its binocular vision to increase depth perception and helps the Chameleon to aim with pin point accuracy.

Extrudable Tongue

Chameleons have very unique tongues which they utilize to catch their prey. A chameleon's tongue is normally 1.5 times the length of the chameleon's body and they expel their tongues at blinding speeds to catch their prey. Most chameleons can expel their tongues in 1/16th of a second which allows them to easily catch a fly in midair.

Color Changing

Some species of chameleon are able to change the coloration and pattern of their skin. The main colors that chameleons utilize while changing their coloring are: pinks, blue, red, green, brown, orange, yellow, purple and turquoise. Chameleons have a superficial layer of skin which contains pigments and underneath this superficial layer there are cells with guanine crystals. The chameleon can change the space between the guanine crystals which manipulates the wavelengths of light that reflect off their skin. The main purpose of a chameleons color change is to camouflage themselves from predators, for temperature control and for social signaling. In terms of social signaling chameleons tend to present themselves in brighter colors when they are being aggressive and darker, more earthy tones, when they are signaling submission.

MOST COMMON SPECIES KEPT AS PETS

As previously mentioned there are over 200 different types of chameleons and they vary in size, color, appearance and rarity. Despite there being multiple types of chameleon only a few are readily available to own as house hold pets due to the fact that some need specialized habitats and may have dispositions that make them unsuitable household pets. The following section will give a general description of the most common types of chameleons that are kept as pets to help you choose which species of chameleon best fits your lifestyle and knowledge. It is best practice to ask for more information about the species you choose to purchase from the reptile store.

Carpet Chameleon

The Carpet chameleon originally come from Madagascar. They are, on average, a smaller species of chameleon. Males normally grow to around 9 inches in length. They have a short life span of between 2 and 3 years. The daytime temperature of their enclosure should be around 75 degrees Fahrenheit and the humidity level should be around 75%. Due to their both their active, docile and hardy nature they are a very common choice for household pets for beginner chameleon keepers.

Four-Horned Chameleon

The Four-horned chameleon originally come from Cameroon. They live for around 5 years and can grow to up to 14 inches in length. During the daytime their enclosure should be heated to around 75 degrees Fahrenheit and the humidity level should be at around 85% which can be tricky to achieve for a beginner chameleon keeper. They are normally chosen to be household pets due to their interesting aesthetic.

Flap-Necked Chameleon

The Flap-necked chameleon originally comes from Africa – primarily both eastern and southern Africa. They normally grow to around 13 inches in length and live for between 2 and 3 years. During the daytime they require their enclosure to be heated to 75 degrees Fahrenheit and for the humidity to be at around 75%. Like the carpet chameleon they have a hardy nature which makes them ideal pets for beginner chameleon keepers.

Fischer's Chameleon

The Fischer's chameleon originally comes from Kenya and Tanzania. They are a moderately sized chameleon and commonly grow to be over 15 inches in length and live up to 3 years. During the daytime their enclosure needs to be heated to 75 degree Fahrenheit and the relative humidity of the enclosure need to change between 75% and 85%. They are more complicated to keep as pets but can do very well if kept under the correct conditions.

Jackson's Chameleon

The Jackson's chameleon originally comes from eastern Africa but was also introduced to Hawaii were wild specimens have flourished. They commonly grow to around 13 inches in length and can live up to 8 years! A daytime temperature of 75 degrees Fahrenheit and a humidity level of between 65% and 75% is required. Due to their interesting three horned appearance and the length of time they live for, the Jackson's chameleon is a very popular household pet.

Meller's Chameleon

The Meller's chameleon originally comes from eastern Africa. They are one of the larger species of chameleon and can grow up to 24 inches in length. They also have a long lifespan of around 12 years. They require a daytime enclosure temperature of 80 degrees Fahrenheit and a humidity level of 70%. They are known to be an aggressive species and are not easy to handle. It is considered best practice to only purchase a Meller's chameleon if you are an experienced chameleon keeper.

Veiled Chameleon

The Veiled chameleon originally comes from Saudi Arabia and Yemen. Males commonly grow to around 24 inches in length and normally live for up to 5 years. They require a daytime enclosure temperature of 80 degrees Fahrenheit and a humidity level of 70%. Veiled chameleons commonly eat plant matter as well as insects. They are very popular household pets due to their docile nature, interesting appearance and ease of feeding.

Panther Chameleon

The Panther chameleon originally comes from the northern regions of Madagascar. Males are dramatically larger than females and normally grow to around 20 inches in length and commonly live for between 5 and 7 years. They require a daytime enclosure temperature of 80 degrees Fahrenheit and a humidity level of 70%. They have a very interesting appearance which many pet owners find attractive. They are also common household pets due to their docile nature which makes handling relatively easy in comparison to other species of chameleon.

Oustalet's Chameleon

The Oustalet's chameleon originally comes from Madagascar. They are very large reptiles and commonly grow to over 30 inches in length! They likewise have a relatively long life span of around 12 years! They require a daytime enclosure temperature of 80 degrees Fahrenheit and a humidity level of 70%. These lizards make very common household pets for owners who want a larger species of chameleon.

CHAMELEONS AS PETS

Chameleons are one of the most popular lizard species to be kept as household pets. As previously mentioned chameleons have an interesting physical appearance and a hardy nature which definitely aids in their popularity. As mentioned above most species of chameleon also have a very docile nature which is a further reason that they make fantastic household pets.

Before Purchase

Before purchasing your chameleon it is best practice to set up and heat your pet's enclosure for a minimum of a week before introducing chameleon into it. This will allow for your enclosure to heat to the desired temperature and for you to check that the lighting and humidity are correct for your chameleon's needs. Setting the enclosure up in advance also allows you to troubleshoot, and resolve, any issues with your set up before purchasing your pet.

Choosing a Chameleon

It is important to consider which species of chameleon is best suited to your lifestyle before purchasing one for a pet. Chameleons are very easily stressed and they need a relaxed environment. It is therefore important to have enough space for their enclosure and to make sure no other household pets, such as cats or dogs, can come into contact with your chameleon. As previously mentioned there are differences in temperament and enclosure requirements. Once you have decided on a species to purchase it is important to also choose a chameleon that looks alert during the purchasing process. As your approach the chameleon enclosure the lizard's eyes should follow you and look both alert and interested. The last thing to check for during the purchasing process is if the chameleon has any visible physical deformities. Physical deformities include burns, sores, pus and external parasites. Some chameleons may have parts of their tails missing but this is not necessarily anything to worry about as long as the wound looks healed and uninfected.

Transporting your Lizard

It is important to know how to correctly transport your lizard as you will need to transport it after purchase and for any visits to the vet. The safest way to transport your lizard is to place your lizard into an appropriately sized and ventilated plastic container. For added comfort, and to further avoid injury, you can line the container with absorbent and soft paper. It is important to keep the transportation container warm. A good way to keep the temperature of the container warm is to use a heat pack during the transportation process. It is best practice to keep transit time to a minimum to reduce the chance of your lizard becoming stressed.

Handling

Handling your chameleon is not needed but can be a fun activity for both your pet and yourself. It is important to remember that every chameleon has its own personality and some chameleons will therefore enjoy handling more than others. Feeding your chameleon by hand is a great way to introduce handling as this will lower the chance of your chameleon acting aggressively towards you due to it associating you with feeding.

Can multiple chameleons be housed together?

It is not considered best practice to house multiple chameleons together. Chameleons are generally solitary and territorial and may be stressed if they have a cage-mate. Males in particular are very likely to become aggressive if they are housed with another chameleon.

Recording

It is highly advisable to keep a record throughout your chameleon's life. By regularly noting down weight, length and feeding patterns you will have a useful resource to help notice any potential problems with your chameleon and to likewise make sure it is in good health.

CAGE AND HABITAT

A pet chameleon requires a fairly elaborate habitat and will need the correct cage, temperature and humidity levels in order to keep your pet happy and healthy. It is important to keep your chameleon's enclosure in a secluded part of your house as excessive noise or human traffic will cause your lizard to become stressed. A positive of a correctly set up and located enclosure is the fact that your chameleon will become more active and entertaining.

Cage

A chameleon cage can be a tall glass terrarium, a large fish tank or a vivarium use for other reptiles. It is important to have a screened or mesh top to avoid any prey escaping the enclosure. Glass terrariums are considered best practice as they allow for optimal temperature and humidity control. When purchasing a juvenile chameleon it is important to take into consideration that your lizard will quickly outgrow a terrarium designed for a juvenile lizard. It is best practice to purchase a large enclosure for your pet from the outset.

No Cage

Some owners prefer to not cage their chameleons and instead opt for leaving their chameleon on a large Ficus Tree. If this is to do done it is important to provide your chameleon with a large tree with branches suitable for walk and leaves suitable to be misted. However it is not considered best practice to provide your chameleon with an open habitat due to the fact that it allows other household pets, or small children, to potentially disturb your chameleon.

A Combination of Both

It is considered best practice to house your chameleon in a terrarium that has a Ficus Tree inside of it. This combination allows for a great replication of the chameleons natural habitat while also providing it with the safety and security it needs to live a stress free life.

Décor

If you do not choose to provide your chameleon with a Ficus Tree inside their enclosure you will need to instead provide your lizard with numerous horizontal branches to climb. It is also important to have an abundance of leaves present within your pets enclosure to provide it with multiple locations to drink droplets and places to hide.

HEATING AND LIGHTING

All species of reptile require a temperature gradient within their vivarium to allow them to select a temperature that best suits their individual needs at any given moment. It is important to optimize both temperature and lighting to create a comfortable habitat for your chameleon.

Primary Heating Source

It is important to place your method of heating on one side of your vivarium to allow for a natural temperature gradient to be created. It is best practice to use an under tank heater (such as the 'Zoo Med Repti Therm U.T.H'). Under tank heaters come in various sizes which allows you to choose the best one to create a temperature gradient within your vivarium. It is likewise important to have a decent thermometer available to check the temperature gradient within your vivarium. It is best practice to use a thermometer which is not fixed to the side of the vivarium. By attaching the thermometer to a wall of the vivarium you will only be measuring the temperature of the air within the tank rather and the temperature of the actual surfaces your lizard resides on. Hot rocks and heat stones are an alternative method of heating your chameleon's vivarium. Hot rocks and heat stones are not considered best practice for heating a reptile vivarium due to the fact that they can potentially become too hot which can lead to the reptile burning themselves. The optimal temperature gradient for a vivarium containing a chameleon is 78 degrees Fahrenheit at the cooler end and 88 degrees Fahrenheit at the warmer end (or between 25 and 31 degrees Celsius).

Secondary Heating Source

A secondary heating source, in the form of a 20-75 watt incandescent bulb in a ceramic case, is a great way to create an area in the vivarium for your lizard to bask. When a bulb is being used as a secondary heat source it is best to place a large flat stone underneath it to allow the lizard to bask comfortably. It is likewise important to place the bulb out of reach of your lizard as they may burn themselves against the hot bulbs surface.

Lighting

Reptiles are reliant on natural daylight to set their day and night patterns. Natural sunlight contains UV (ultraviolet) light in two forms, UVa and UVb, that are essential to a chameleon's wellbeing. Firstly chameleons use UVa to be able to see color. Secondly they use UVb to produce essential vitamin D3 in their skin. D3 is used to store calcium which is an essential mineral for the lizard's health as it prevent metabolic bone disease. UVb does not pass through glass windows and therefore a specialized reptile UVb lamp must be used inside the vivarium itself. You can use either fluorescent or mercury vapor bulbs for your reptile lamp. Fluorescent bulbs need to be replaced every six months as their UVb output diminishes over time. It is important to check that the bulb you choose for your lamp has at least 5 percent UVb (you can locate this information on the lightbulb's packaging. It is important to create a 'photo gradient,' from light to shade, within your vivarium that matches the temperature gradient. Chameleons need between 12 and 14 hours of light each day and it is therefore important to remember to turn the reptile light off each night to simulate night.

Brumation

Brumation is a natural energy saving process and is common within adult chameleons during the cooler months. It serves a very similar process to hibernation. Brumation is triggered by a reduction in temperature. Chameleons will normally eat less and sleep more during this process and it is best practice to closely monitor your lizard during this time.

FEEDING AND WATERING YOUR PET

Chameleons are relatively easy to provide for in terms of food and water which makes them an excellent pet for beginner lizard owners. The feeding process is made easier by the fact that their primary food sources are easily obtainable. However the following section will discuss, and explain, some important tips to help optimize the feeding process to keep your lizard as healthy as possible.

What do Chameleons Eat?

As previously mentioned chameleons are insectivore which means that their mainly consist of insects. It is not uncommon for chameleons to also eat plant matter on occasions. It is best practice to feed juvenile lizards on a diet consisting of mainly insects to help them grow. It is also not uncommon for owners to feed larger chameleons pinkies (baby mice).

How much do Chameleons Eat?

An adult chameleon should be fed on between 30 and 50 crickets (or similar sized insects) a week. Best practice for feeding your pet would be in twos: one day feed your chameleon insects and one day feed it nothing. A juvenile chameleon should be fed more often than adult chameleons and it is considered best practice to leave around 10 crickets in your chameleons cage at all times.

Pros and Cons of Crickets

The main pros of using crickets as the your pets main food source is the fact that they are nutritionally superior to mealworms and are likewise more active prey which creates a more stimulating feeding process for your chameleon. However there are multiple downsides to using crickets as your primary prey choice. Buying crickets in bulk means that you will have to worry about looking after the crickets before using them as prey (which means providing them with food and water). Likewise it is important to note that any large amounts of crickets will produce a significant amount of noise due to their consistent chirping. Another potential negative of using crickets as your primary food choice is the fact that they can easily escape either from the chameleon's vivarium or the cage you are keeping the crickets in before they are used as prey. Lastly it is also possible for uneaten crickets to eat your chameleon's fecal matter, which will contain harmful parasites, which will then be transferred to your chameleon during the feeding process.

Pros and Cons of Mealworms

The main pro of using mealworms as your pet's main source of prey is the fact that they are not very active, they are unable to jump or climb, which means that there is virtually no chance of them escaping. A further benefit of using mealworms is the fact that they can be refrigerated for weeks on end which means that you do not need to worry about feeding and looking after your lizard's prey. It is common practice to server mealworms to your chameleon in a small tray which simultaneously eliminates any chance of the worms ingesting the chameleon's fecal matter. The tray likewise makes it possible to provide your chameleon with a tray of worms on a weekly basis simplifying the feeding process. However there are some negatives of using mealworms. Firstly, as previously mentioned, they are of less nutritional value than crickets and a far less stimulating prey for your lizard. It is possible to increase mealworms activity by introducing a small piece of vegetable to the tray that you place the meal worms in. The introduction of a vegetable allows the mealworms to move around and feed which will help to create a stimulating feeding process for your lizard. Similarly the exoskeleton of mealworms is potentially harder to digest than the exoskeleton of crickets.

Gut Loading

The process of 'gut loading' involves feeding your prey of choice before feeding them to your chameleon. The purpose of gut loading is to increase the nutritional value of the prey by feeding them food high in nutrients to transfer the nutrient to your chameleon once the prey has been eaten. It is common to feed both crickets and mealworms carrots, oranges, pears and other vegetables for the purpose of gut loading. If you are using mealworms as your prey of choice it is best practice to place your gut loading food in the tray with the worms when you introduce them into the vivarium. This will allow for the mealworms to always be gut loaded and there is a possibility that your chameleon will ingest the gut loading food directly while it ingests the mealworms.

Dusting the Prey

It is possible to dust your prey of choice in powders that contain important vitamins and nutrients. To dust your prey of choice effectively place the prey and the powder in either a small can or small bag and shake gently to coat the prey's body in the powder. It is important to shake gently as you do not wish to kill the prey as this may make the chameleon disinterested in eating it. It is likewise important to make sure that the prey does not have copious amounts of dust on its body to avoid the chance of dust getting into your lizard's eyes which could lead to an infection.

Pinkies and Waxworms

Both pinkies and waxworms are high in calories and are therefore a great way to increase your chameleon's weight if they are underweight. It is common for chameleons to lose weight during periods of sickness and it is not uncommon for female chameleons to lose weight during the breeding process – primarily after they have laid their eggs. Both pinkies and waxworms should not be the main source of feeding for your lizard as it is possible for chameleons to become obese which leads to multiple health problems.

Plant Based Food

Some chameleons will eat plant based matter on a regular basis while others will only eat it on occasions – it best to keep a record of what your pet eats so you can feed it depending on its temperament. The best greens and vegetables to include in a salad for your chameleon are: watercress, rocket, cress, dandelion, clover, red and green bell peppers, green beans, acorn squash, lentils, peas, pumpkin, plantain leaves, grated butternut squash and parsley. It is best to avoid giving your chameleon

kale, cabbage and spinach as too much will prevent
calcium absorption and can create a hormonal
imbalance within your lizard. Spraying your vegetables
and greens with water before serving them to your
lizard helps them stay fresh for longer. It is best practice
to shred your vegetables and salad into a mixture to
help encourage your chameleon to eat a variety of food.

Not Eating?

You should not be alarmed if your chameleon does
not eat every day. It is not uncommon for chameleons to
not eat for up to three days during the shedding process.
However if your lizard has not eaten for three days and
there is no sign of the shedding process taking place it is
best to take your lizard to the vet to make sure that it is
not ill.

Watering

Chameleons prefer to drink water in droplets form
rather than use a water bowl. A water mister on a timer
works well in terms of supplying your pet with water. It
is important to aim your water mister at the leaves
within the enclosure to allow droplets to form. A dripper
is a good alternative to a mister. A dripper will
periodically drop water onto leaves within the enclosure
to allow your chameleon to drink It is also possible to

provide your chameleon with water using a hand water spray. Your spray bottle should always be full of fresh water. While hand spraying your enclosure it is again important to aim the spray at leaves or the chameleon itself as they are able to lick the droplets of their own bodies. It is important to check that your source of water for your pet is not disturbing the humidity levels required to best care for your lizard.

SHEDDING

Like all reptiles and amphibians, most species of chameleon will periodically shed their skin. Chameleons will not shed their entire skin in a single shedding process but will rather shed their skin in large pieces. Juvenile chameleons will shed their skin much more frequently than adult chameleons due to the fact that they are still growing and will need to shed their skin as they outgrow it.

How to tell if your Chameleon is about to Shed

If your chameleon's coloring has suddenly become duller do not worry. The dulling of skin is a good indicator that your lizard is about to shed its skin and the shedding process should occur within a few days of the dulling process. Do not pull off old skin if it seems stuck as it may damage or pull off new skin forming underneath. If your chameleon has a lot of unshed skin it is best practice to bathe your chameleon to help loosen the old skin.

A Moist Shelter

A moist shelter can be provided during the shedding process as it provides a higher level of humidity which assists the chameleon in the shedding process. A good example of a moist shelter is a Tupperware container lined with cypress mulch or peat moss to create the moisture. If you are planning on introducing a moist shelter during the shedding process it is imperative to make sure that the humidity level of your vivarium does not change dramatically.

FINAL THOUGHTS

Thank you for purchasing our pet care manual on caring for a chameleon. We hope you have found the information both interesting and informative. We hope that this book has allowed you to make an informed choice on whether owning a chameleon suits you and if so we hope that the information will help you to provide the best quality care for your pet chameleon.

We will be publishing multiple other pet care manuals on our author page on Kindle. If you have an interest in exotic and exciting pets then we highly suggest you check out our other work.

I am passionate about providing the best quality information to our customers. We would highly appreciate any feedback, or reviews, you could leave us on our Kindle page to allow us to help create the best possible pet care products available on the market.

Tabitha Jones

Printed in Great Britain
by Amazon

56293322R00026